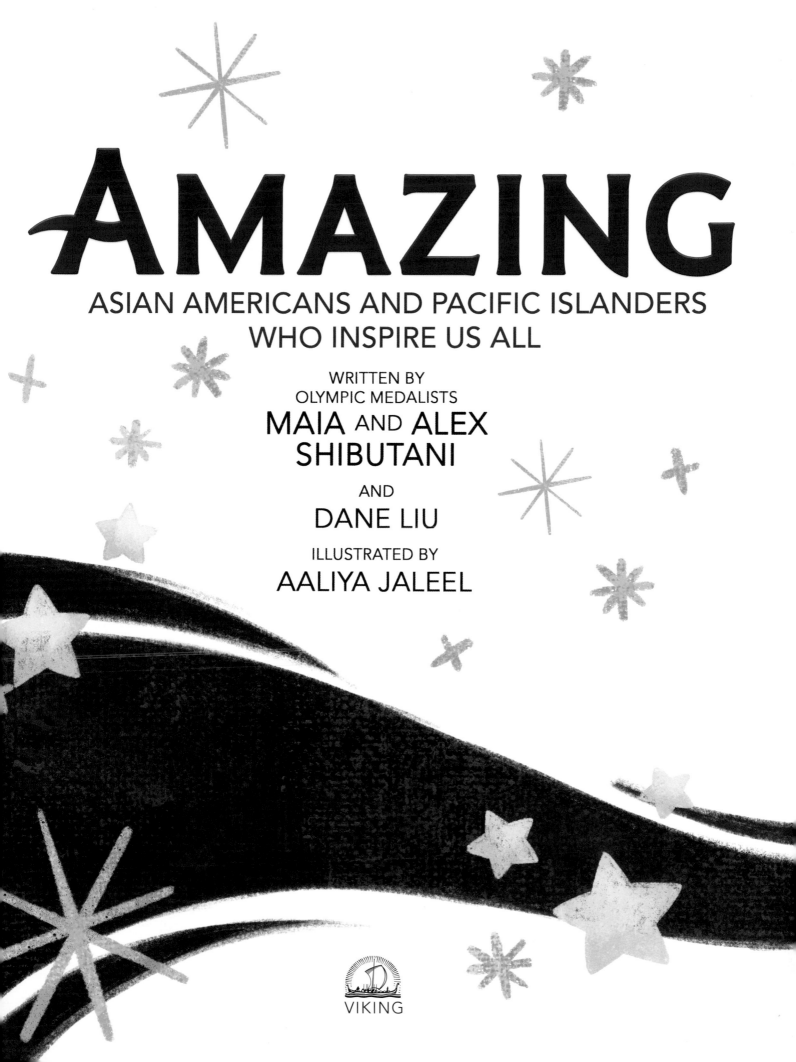

AMAZING

ASIAN AMERICANS AND PACIFIC ISLANDERS
WHO INSPIRE US ALL

WRITTEN BY
OLYMPIC MEDALISTS
MAIA AND **ALEX**
SHIBUTANI

AND

DANE LIU

ILLUSTRATED BY

AALIYA JALEEL

VIKING

VIKING
An imprint of Penguin Random House LLC, New York

First published in the United States of America by Viking,
an imprint of Penguin Random House LLC, 2023

Visit us online at penguinrandomhouse.com.

Library of Congress Cataloging-in-Publication Data is available.

Manufactured in Italy

ISBN 9780593525432

3 5 7 9 10 8 6 4 2

LEG

Design by Opal Roengchai
Text set in Ambigue and KG All of Me

For the next generation of leaders, storytellers, and innovators . . .
This book is a little inspiration and encouragement from us to you.
—M. S. & A. S.

To my kids and all kids—these are your stories; this is your history.
—D. L.

For my teachers, who supported and guided me toward my goals.
—A. J.

WONG KIM ARK

In 1895, Kim Ark was coming home after a trip to China. From the steamship, he could peer at the familiar hills of San Francisco, where he was born. But at the port, officials detained him, saying he wasn't American. Kim Ark knew they were wrong. He fought his case all the way to the Supreme Court, where he won. Today, thanks to Wong Kim Ark, any child born in the United States is a citizen, no matter their race.

DR. MABEL PING-HUA LEE

Ten thousand people marched through New York City in 1912 in one of the largest protests for women's suffrage. Helping lead the pack was sixteen-year-old Mabel. Even though Chinese immigrants like her could not become citizens or vote, Mabel still fought for the cause, believing that voting for good leaders would open more doors for women. She devoted her life to education and civil rights for all.

DUKE KAHANAMOKU AND CARISSA MOORE

Surfing made its debut at the 2020 Olympic Games, and Carissa became the first woman to win a gold medal. For Native Hawaiians, surfing is not only a sport but also an important part of their culture. A century before, Duke—a three-time Olympic swim champion— had asked the Olympic Committee to include surfing, but they refused. So he traveled to share the art of wave riding with the world. Carissa's historic win was a dream come true for her and her hero Duke.

VICTORIA MANALO DRAVES AND DR. SAMMY LEE

When Vicki and Sammy were kids in California, public pools were for "whites only." Vicki, who was part Filipino, and Sammy, who was Korean American, could only use the pools once a week, right before they were drained. Because of this, Sammy mostly practiced diving in a backyard sandpit. Vicki convinced a club to let her in, and she dived up to one hundred times each practice. At the 1948 Olympic Games, Vicki and Sammy triumphed, becoming the first Asian Americans to win gold medals.

Growing up in the early 1900s in Los Angeles, Anna would visit movie sets and mimic the scenes in her mirror. At seventeen years old, she dazzled Hollywood with her acting and became the first Chinese American movie star. Despite her talent, Anna was given small roles while the leading Asian parts were played by white actors wearing offensive makeup. Anna spoke up about racism and representation. She appeared in over sixty films and received a star on the Hollywood Walk of Fame. In 2022, she was honored on the US quarter.

BRUCE LEE

Born in 1940 in San Francisco, Bruce grew up in Hong Kong. He studied martial arts and honed his skills in public matches on rooftops. His unique style and charisma catapulted him into action movies, where he thrilled audiences as the first Asian American action star. Everyone wanted to be like Bruce, but he believed in the importance of being true to oneself. As an actor, choreographer, storyteller, and teacher, Bruce has inspired millions of people all over the world.

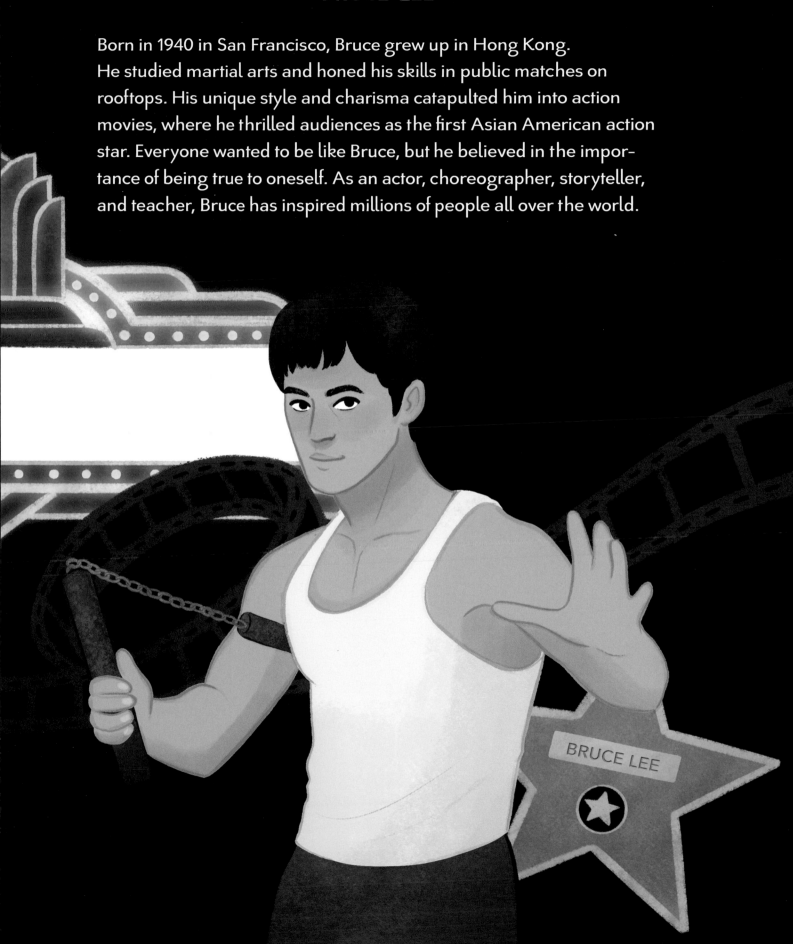

BRUCE LEE

YOUNG KWOK "CORKY" LEE

As a Chinese American teenager, Corky saw a historic photograph celebrating the completion of the Transcontinental Railroad. But something was missing. While most of the workers had been Chinese, none of them were included in the picture. This discovery inspired Corky to dedicate his life's work to photography and documenting the stories of Asian Americans and Pacific Islanders. In 2014, Corky famously re-created the railroad photo with many descendants of the workers. He said, "Every time I take my camera out of my bag, it's like drawing a sword to combat indifference, injustice, and discrimination."

LARRY ITLIONG AND PHILIP VERA CRUZ

Larry and Philip united communities as they led a key labor movement in US history. For years, Filipino and Latino grape pickers in California faced low wages and no benefits. In 1965, Larry and Philip organized the Filipino workers to strike. Though farm bosses had defeated prior strikes by pitting the two groups against each other, Larry invited Cesar Chavez and the Latino workers to join in. This partnership succeeded and helped create America's first farmworkers union, which still protects workers today.

HELEN ZIA

Helen was born in New Jersey, but people treated her like a foreigner. These early experiences of racism compelled Helen to find her voice as a journalist and civil rights activist. In 1982, a fellow Chinese American named Vincent Chin was murdered in a hate crime, yet his killers were released without jail time. Helen spoke up. She rallied Asian Americans and other groups to fight racism and demand justice—together. Today, Helen continues to advocate for equity and human rights.

ALICE WONG

Growing up in the 1970s, Alice struggled to belong. She was usually the only disabled person and Chinese American in her class. Today she is a disability activist. While one in five people in the US lives with a disability, they are rarely represented in popular culture. Alice founded the Disability Visibility Project, an online community that grows their voices in the media. She writes, "By recognizing how disabled people enrich our communities, we can all be empowered to make sure disabled people are included."

DANIEL INOUYE

In 1959, Daniel was the first Japanese American elected to Congress. To take the oath, he was asked to raise his right hand, but he could not. Years before, as an American soldier in World War II, Daniel led an attack on an enemy post and lost his right arm. With his left, he hurled a grenade and destroyed the target. After the war, he served the people of Hawaii in the House and the Senate for more than fifty years. Today, Daniel is remembered for all the ways he changed history.

TAMMY DUCKWORTH

Tammy has achieved many firsts: she is the first Thai American elected to the Senate, the first sitting senator to give birth, and the first female member of Congress to use a wheelchair. As a Black Hawk pilot in the Iraq War, Tammy flew combat missions. In 2004, her helicopter was shot down, causing the loss of both legs and damage to her right arm. Today, she is a fierce advocate for working families, disabled people, and veterans' rights, saying, "My aim is to do things that really matter to other people's lives."

KAMALA HARRIS

Kamala is the forty-ninth US vice president—the first woman, first Black person, and first Asian to hold the office. For her victory speech, she wore white, a color of the women's rights movement, to link generations of suffragists like Mabel Lee to the historic moment. Born to Black and Indian American parents, Kamala's fight for civil rights began early, when she went to protests as a young child. While she is the first Madam Vice President, Kamala says, "I will not be the last!"

Until all of us are equal, none of us are equal.

IWAO TAKAMOTO

Iwao was a designer and illustrator of many beloved cartoon characters. He learned to draw while he and other Japanese Americans were unjustly incarcerated during World War II. Once he was free, Iwao filled his notebooks with sketches and brought them to Disney Studios to find a job. There, he worked on several classic films, including *One Hundred and One Dalmatians* and *Cinderella*. Later on, he designed the main characters from the ever-popular *Scooby-Doo*. Today, Iwao's timeless characters continue to delight the world.

ROBERT "BOBBY" LOPEZ

Growing up in a Filipino American family, Bobby started playing the piano when he was six years old and soon after wrote his first song, "Oy Vey, What a Day!" Since then he has composed many unforgettable hits for Disney's animated musicals, such as "Let It Go" from *Frozen* and "Remember Me" from *Coco*. Music and family go hand in hand for Bobby. He and his wife, Kristen, co-created the songs, and their daughters sang in *Frozen*. As a songwriter for movies, television, and theater, Bobby has connected people of all ages to the magic of music.

H.E.R.

H.E.R. stands for "Having Everything Revealed." Growing up, H.E.R.'s favorite pastime was to play music and listen to songs with her dad. As a child, her soulful voice enchanted audiences at the Apollo Theater and on national television. Today, she continues to sing and write songs. H.E.R. has been recognized for her work with many awards, including Grammys and an Oscar! Many of her inspiring and poetic lyrics speak out against racism and injustice. "Music is power," she says, and a way to fight for what's right.

YO-YO MA

In 1962, Yo-Yo was just seven years old when he played the cello for Presidents John F. Kennedy and Dwight D. Eisenhower. Today, he is one of the greatest cellists of all time! He founded the Silk Road Ensemble, featuring artists from different countries and musical traditions. He also created the Bach Project, performing in concerts around the globe and inviting local communities to share ideas for a better world. Yo-Yo harnesses the power of music to connect humanity, build understanding, and change the future.

DR. KALPANA CHAWLA

Growing up in India, Kalpana dreamed of flying. She came to the US to study aerospace engineering and worked her way up to NASA. In 1997, she became the first Indian American woman to fly in outer space. On her second mission, the space shuttle *Columbia* tragically broke apart and Kalpana never came home to Earth. She is remembered for pushing boundaries and achieving her dreams. "When you look at the stars and the galaxy," she said, "you feel that you are not just from any particular piece of land, but from the solar system."

DR. FAZLUR RAHMAN KHAN

What's the tallest building you know? A structural engineer named Fazlur made skyscrapers possible. Born in 1929 in Bangladesh, Fazlur came to the US to study structural engineering before working in Chicago. As he designed, Fazlur would imagine that he was the building, feeling the twists and pulls of winds and gravity. It helped him invent a new way of bracing high-rises against these strong forces. In 1974, he applied his revolutionary design to the 110-story Sears Tower. Thanks to his principles, Fazlur has forever defined urban skylines around the world.

PRABAL GURUNG

As a child, Prabal would play wearing a cape like his favorite superhero, Wonder Woman. Today, he is a fashion designer whose beautiful clothes have been worn by such luminaries as First Lady Michelle Obama. He is also an activist who uses his fashion shows to start conversations about equality; casts models of different races and body sizes; and makes most of his clothes in New York. He co-founded Shikshya Foundation Nepal, which helps provide education to underserved children in the country of his ancestors. For Prabal, fashion is a way to spark change and fight for justice.

VIET THANH NGUYEN

Viet's writing is inspired by his life. In 1975, at four years old, he and his family came to Pennsylvania as war refugees from Vietnam. Now a Pulitzer Prize–winning writer, Viet tells the overlooked stories of America, racism, and people displaced by war. "All wars are fought twice," Viet once said, "the first time on the battlefield, the second time in memory." He writes about those memories, challenging us to look at the truths about our past.

MIN JIN LEE

Min moved to New York from South Korea in 1976 when she was seven years old. She had a hard time making friends and found comfort in reading. As an adult, her passion for stories led her to write her first book. Today, Min is an acclaimed author. She says that writing is her activism, shedding light on the lives of outsiders and people without power. Her works invite readers to cross borders, exercise compassion, and better understand each other.

DWAYNE "THE ROCK" JOHNSON

Few people have succeeded in as many arenas as Dwayne. The Black Samoan businessman is also a pop culture icon, a former football player and wrestler, and one of the biggest movie stars on the planet. Born in 1972, Dwayne grew up in a poor family that moved a lot. Those difficult early years taught him how to connect with people. Dwayne believes the way to succeed is simple, saying, "Be humble. Be hungry. And always be the hardest worker in the room."

MINDY KALING

When Mindy was little, comedy and laughter made her feel less shy. At twenty-four, she was the only woman and person of color on the writing team of *The Office*, a popular TV show. Then she created *The Mindy Project* and became one of the first Indian American TV stars. Today, Mindy is an entertainment legend, writing empowered female characters who refuse to see themselves as the underdogs—like the creator herself. Asked why she is so confident, Mindy answered, "Why wouldn't I be?"

SUNISA "SUNI" LEE

At the 2020 Olympic Games, Suni was the first Hmong American Olympian and the first Asian American to win the gold medal in the all-around gymnastics competition. Just months before, Suni had broken her foot, lost relatives to illness, and grappled with an accident that seriously injured her dad. But she persevered with a spirit that characterizes the Hmong American community—most of whom, like her parents, braved dangerous journeys to the US as refugees. Suni dedicates her victories to them.

JULIE CHU

In 2014, Julie carried the United States flag at the Closing Ceremony of the Olympic Winter Games. She is a four-time Olympic medalist, five-time world champion, and the first Asian American on the US women's hockey team. When Julie was young, her hometown in Connecticut didn't have a girls' team, so Julie played with the boys. Now one of the finest athletes in Team USA history, she coaches the next generation and works to make hockey more inclusive.

CHUCK AOKI

Chuck's first word was "ball," which was a sign of his future love of sports. Born with a rare genetic condition, Chuck began by playing wheelchair basketball. Then, at age fifteen, he discovered wheelchair rugby. *Crash, slam!* He was hooked right away. At the 2020 Paralympic Games in Tokyo, Chuck was chosen to lead Team USA at the Opening Ceremony as a flag-bearer. He has won three Paralympic medals and advocates for representation, equality, and the support of future parasports.

CRISTETA "CRIS" COMERFORD

Cris is the executive chef at the most famous house in America: The White House. Born in the Philippines, Cris grew up with the comforting aromas of her family's kitchen, where cooking was a way to say "I love you." She came to the US when she was twenty-three years old and dreamed of becoming a chef. Her first job was making salads, and from there she worked and learned in many restaurants. Now she is the first woman and the first Asian American to serve as the official top chef to at least four presidents.

DAVID CHANG

Born in Virginia, Dave grew up savoring the Korean cooking of his immigrant family. As an adult, his passion for food
took him to other countries, where he learned about many
cuisines. Today, Dave is an award-winning chef whose
restaurants, books, podcast, and TV shows have redefined
American dining. "We tell stories through food," Dave says.
His inventive dishes connect cultures and show how deli-
cious different foods can be. In these ways, the stories he
tells are those of an evolving America.

ELIZABETH CHAI VASARHELYI AND JIMMY CHIN

When Chai and Jimmy first met, Chai was a film director, producer, and writer. Jimmy was a climber, skier, photographer, and cinematographer. By combining their different skills and experiences, they have told unique stories. In their movies, such as *Free Solo* and *The Rescue*, Chai and Jimmy share the enduring beauty of the human spirit and introduce us to earth's natural wonders. The two storytellers are also parents and partners in life.

MAYA LIN

Born in 1959, Maya grew up in Ohio and loved exploring nature in the woods around her home. She later studied architecture, a field with few women. At just twenty-one years old, Maya won the design contest for the Vietnam Veterans Memorial, which is celebrated as a place to reflect and heal. She went on to design many structures that tell the story of America, including recent projects about climate change. Maya's work has helped Americans experience art and understand past, present, and future.

KATHY JETÑIL-KIJINER

Kathy is a poet and performance artist from the Marshall Islands. As rising sea levels threaten to wipe out Pacific islands like hers, she focuses her work on climate change. One of Kathy's poems, performed at a United Nations Climate Summit, is written to her baby daughter. It foretells a grim future: their people fleeing, their homeland lost to the sea. To prevent this, the global community must work together now. Using her art, Kathy fights to save our planet—for her family, her nation, and all of humanity.

AUTHORS' NOTES

This all started with a wish. We wished that we had a book like this on our shelf when we were kids. It would've helped us understand at an earlier age that we should embrace the qualities that set us apart. It was gratifying to discover that there were passionate people who shared our hopes and vision for this book. Together, we have created this collection to celebrate thirty-six historic and contemporary Asian Americans and Pacific Islanders. Researching these trailblazers was enlightening because we weren't previously familiar with all of them. As we learned more, we became more motivated, and there was greater purpose to our work.

To our readers:
Open your imaginations! Be inspired by these unique individuals who persevered not only for themselves, but for others. Feel heartened by this beautiful community. We encourage you to do more research, share these stories, and pursue your own dreams. We believe in you!

Much love,
Maia and Alex

I've learned a lot writing this book. The stories of these Asian Americans and Pacific Islanders illuminate the history of our country and the world. These thirty-six people have contributed in different ways and at different times, but they share something deeply important. All of them have dreamed, persisted, and overcome. They've built partnerships and devoted their lives to raising awareness and understanding. They've dedicated their lives to making the world fairer and more just. I hope their stories invite you to learn more about Asian Americans and Pacific Islanders. I hope they inspire you to dig deeper and discover the diverse communities that unite us. And I hope they empower you to stretch your imagination, to speak up, and to make choices that respect all people and this planet we call home.

With love and respect,
Dane